I Can Learn

Maths Skills

Written by David Kirkby
Illustrated by John Haslam

 This book belongs to
....

EGMONT

 # Tips for happy home learning

Make learning fun by working at your child's pace and always giving tasks which s/he can do. Tasks that are too difficult will discourage her/him from trying again.

Give encouragement and praise and remember to award gold stars and sticker badges for effort as well as good work.

Always do too little rather than too much, and finish each session on a positive note.

Don't work when you or your child is tired or hungry.

Reinforce workbook activities and new ideas by making use of real objects around the home.

EGMONT
We bring stories to life

Copyright © 2005 Egmont Books Limited
All rights reserved.
Published in Great Britain by Egmont Books Limited,
239 Kensington High Street, London W8 6SA
www.egmont.co.uk

Printed in Italy.
ISBN 1 4052 1561 5
2 4 6 8 10 9 7 5 3 1

Counting to 10

Count and write down the number of spots on each card.

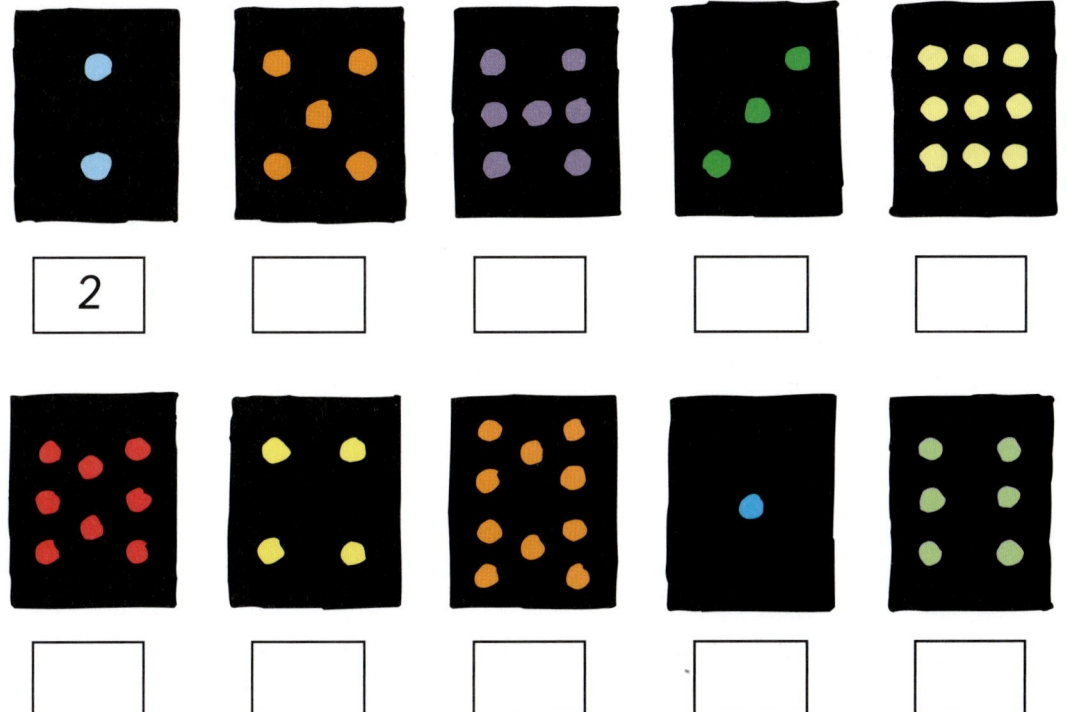

Draw sweets in each jar to match the number on the lid.

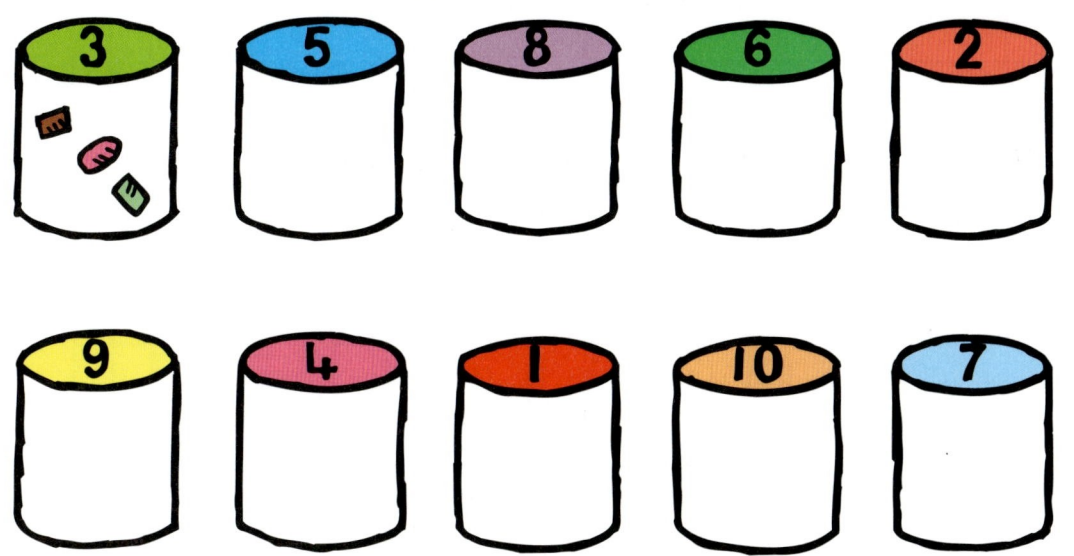

Great drawing. Have a star.

4 Counting to 20

Count and write down the number of oranges in each box

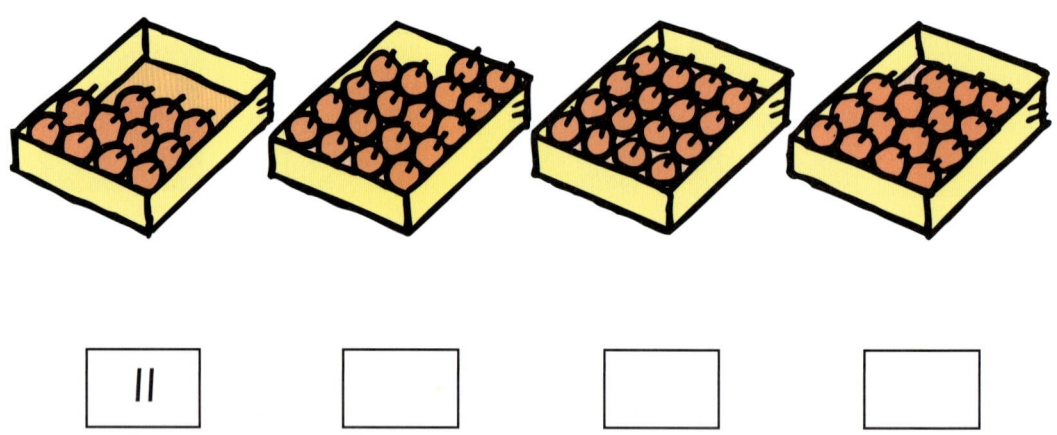

| 11 | | | |

Colour red the number of squares written in the box below

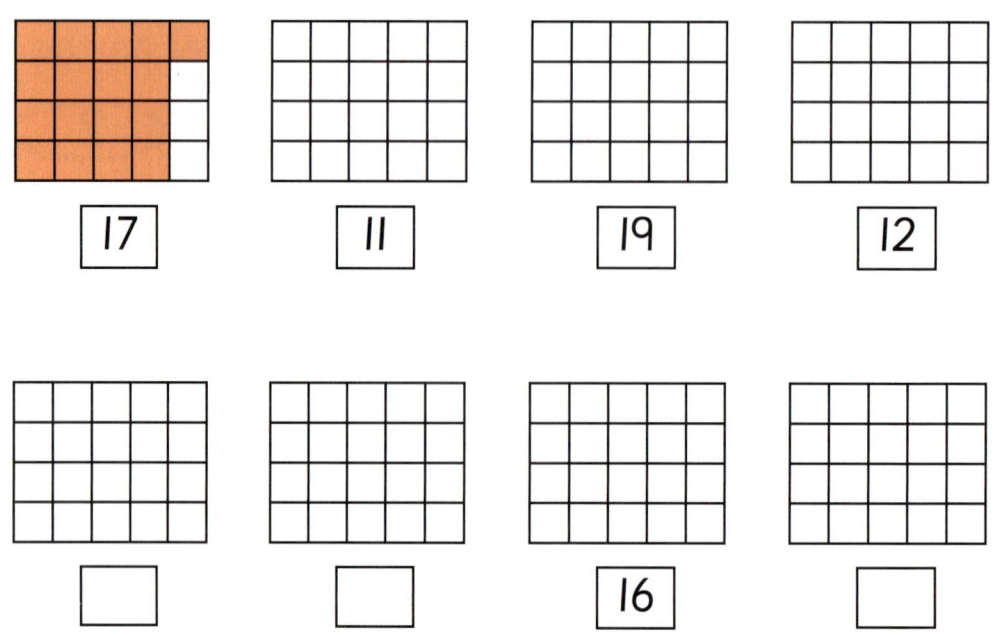

Keep on counting!

Ordering

Write in the missing numbers.

| 1 | 2 | 3 | | 5 | | | 8 | | 10 |

| 7 | 8 | | | 11 | | 13 | | | 16 |

| 17 | | 15 | | 13 | | | 10 | | 8 |

| 20 | | | 17 | | | | | 12 | |

Write the numbers, in order, on the strips.

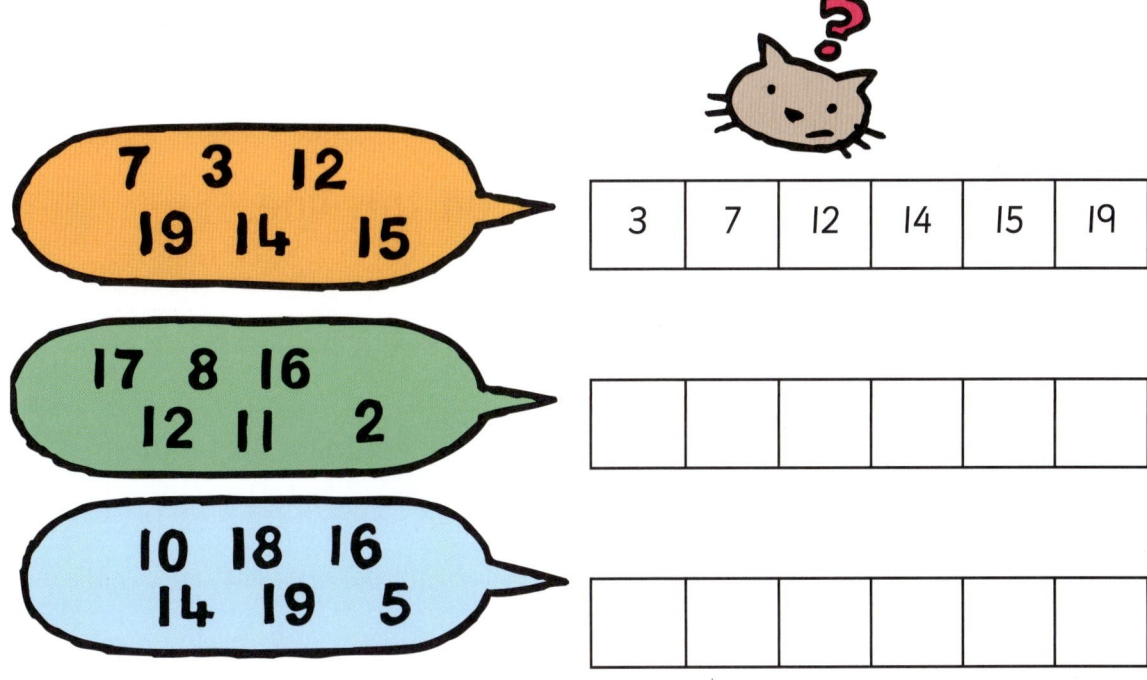

Note for parents: Using number lines and number squares is a useful way of learning about the order of numbers.

6 Number lines

Write the position of each letter on the line.

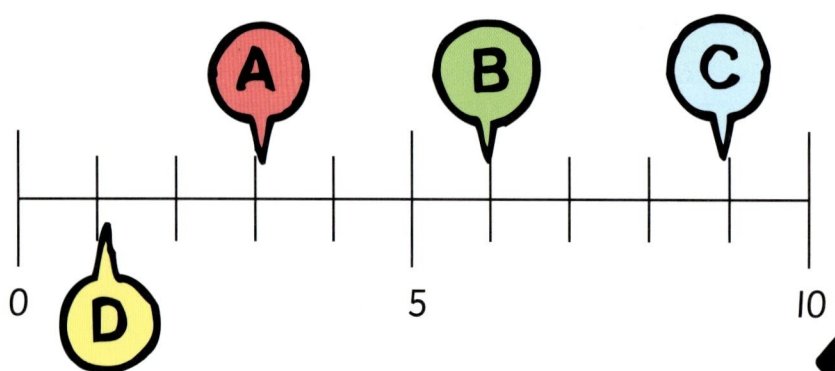

A =
B =
C =
D = ☐

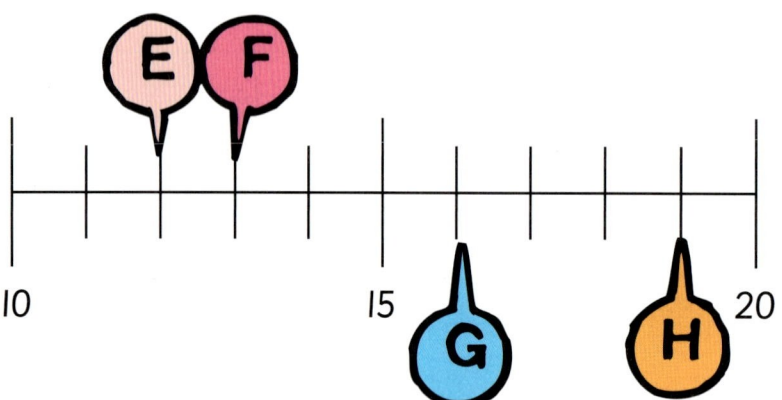

E =
F =
G =
H = ☐

Mark the position of each letter on this line.

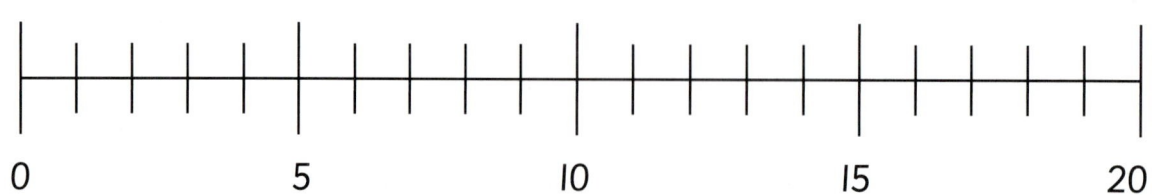

A = 3   B = 7   C = 11   D = 15   E = 18
F = 5   G = 9   H = 12   I = 16   J = 19

Brilliant maths!

Time: o'clock

Write the time under each clock.

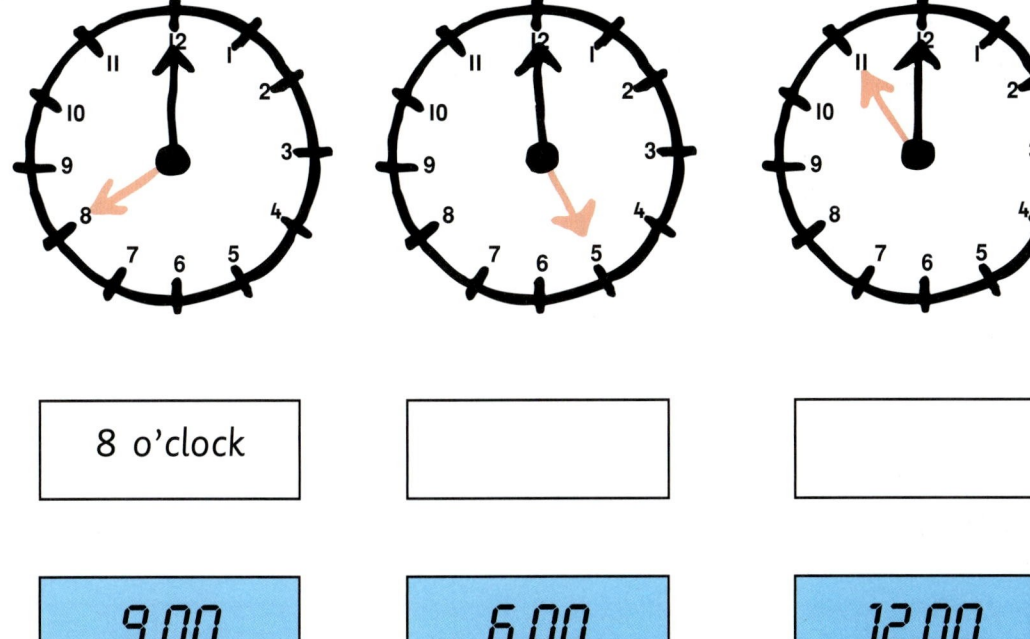

8 o'clock		
9.00	6.00	12.00

Now draw the hands on these clocks.

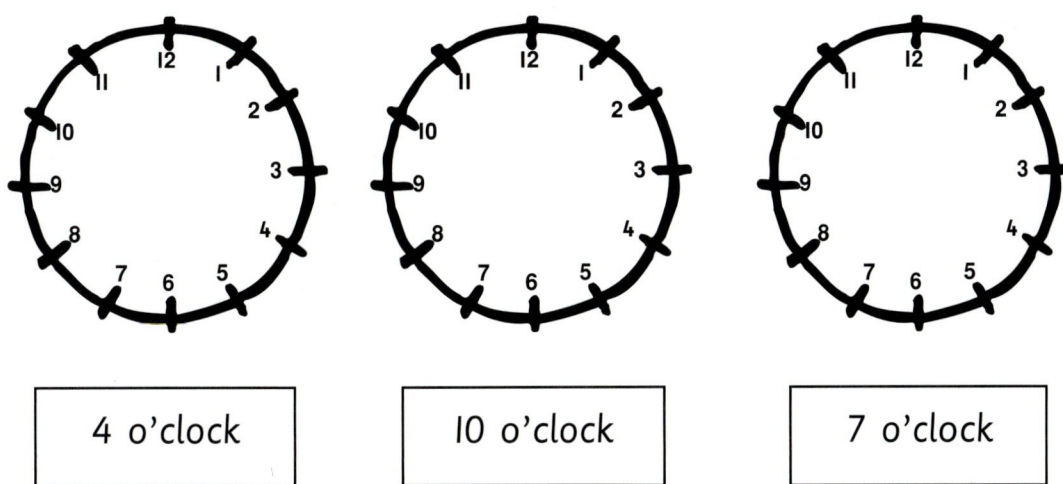

| 4 o'clock | 10 o'clock | 7 o'clock |

Note for parents: Help your child look for digital and analogue time displays around the home.

8 Time: half past

Write the time under each clock.

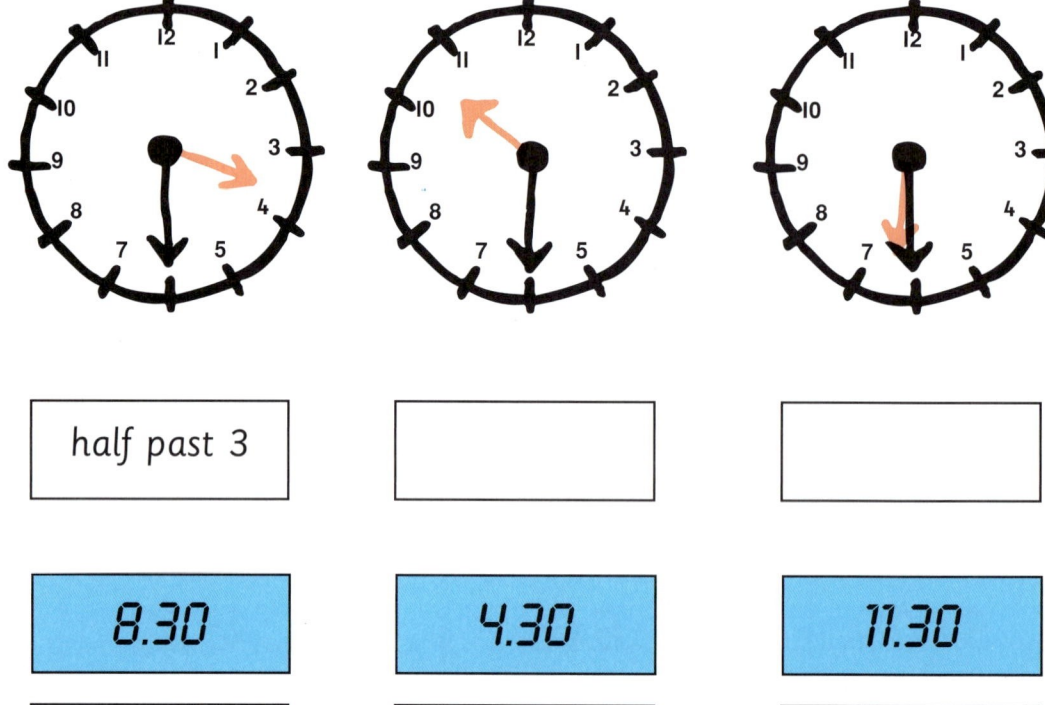

half past 3

8.30   4.30   11.30

Draw the hands on the clocks.

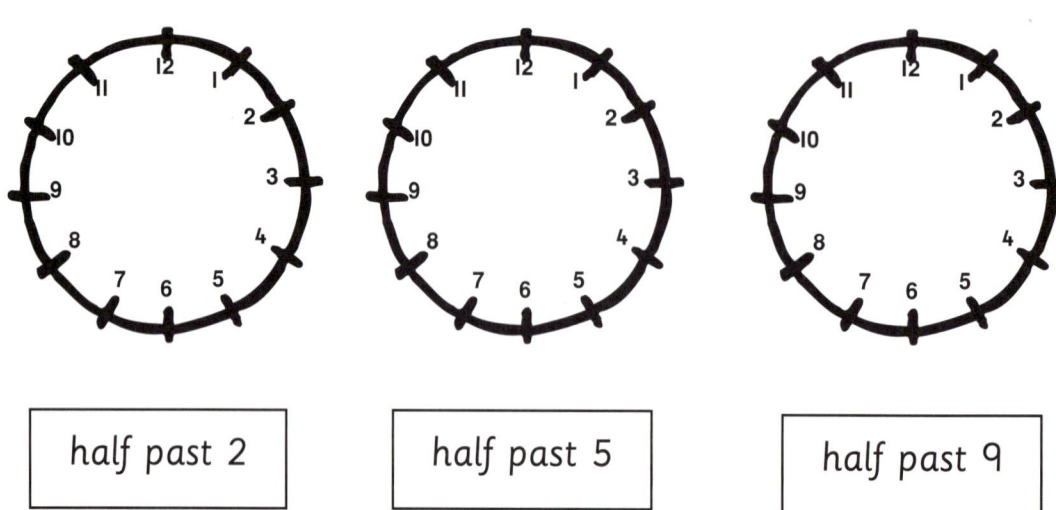

half past 2   half past 5   half past 9

Note for parents: Practise lots of o'clock and half past times with your child before moving on to trickier readings.

Measuring with centimetres

Write down the length of each line in centimetres (cm).

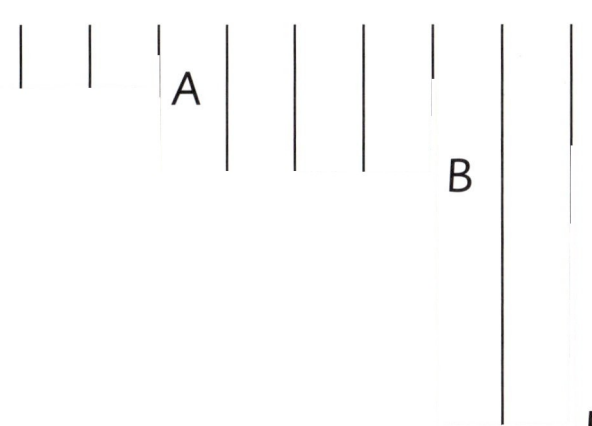

A = ☐ cm

B = ☐ cm

C = ☐ cm

D = ☐ cm

E = ☐ cm

Write the letters, in order, from shortest to longest. ☐☐☐☐☐

Use a ruler to measure the lengths of these lines in centimetres (cm).

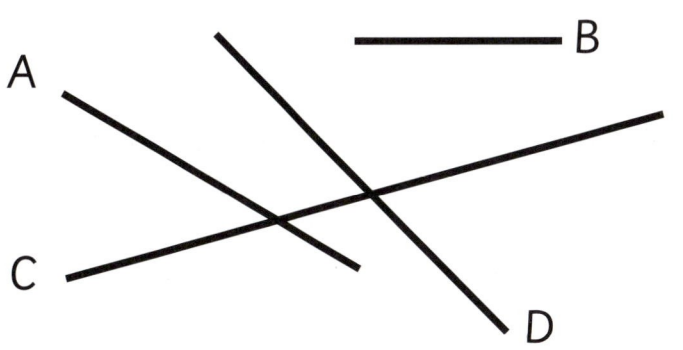

A = ☐ cm

B = ☐ cm

C = ☐ cm

D = ☐ cm

Note for parents: Keep a record of your child's height and weight, which you can update every birthday or six months.

Money

Colour **two** coins which make each amount.

3p

7p

12p

15p

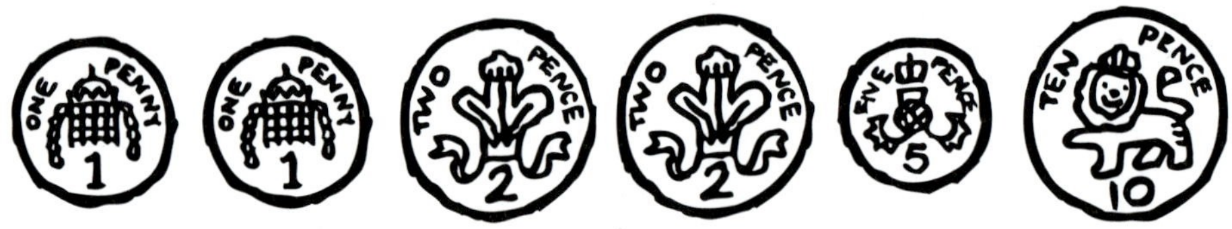

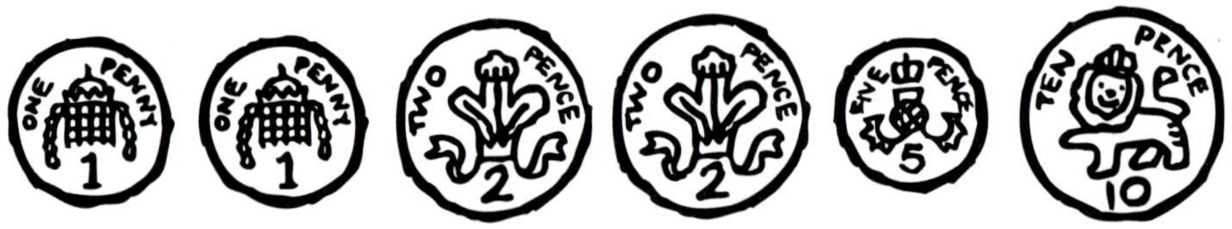

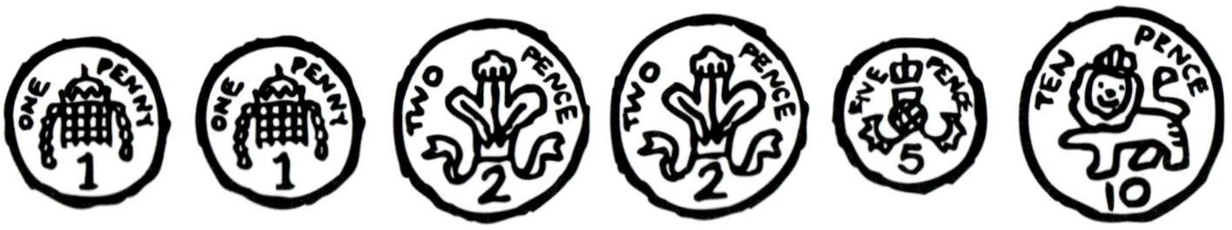

Write **three** coins which make these amounts.

13p	10p	2p	1p	**5p**			
20p				**16p**			

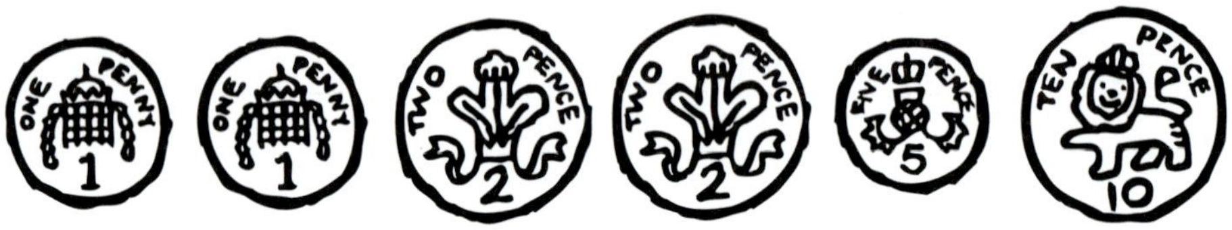

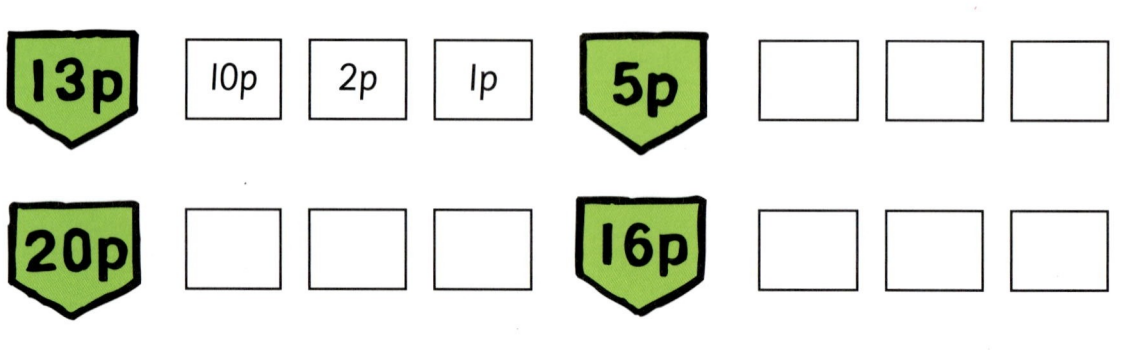

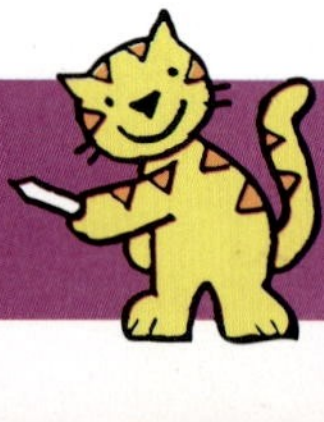

Note for parents: Your child will be asked to solve 'real life' maths problems at school, including using £ and p.

Block graphs

Colour blocks, from the bottom upwards, to show how many there are of each shape.

number

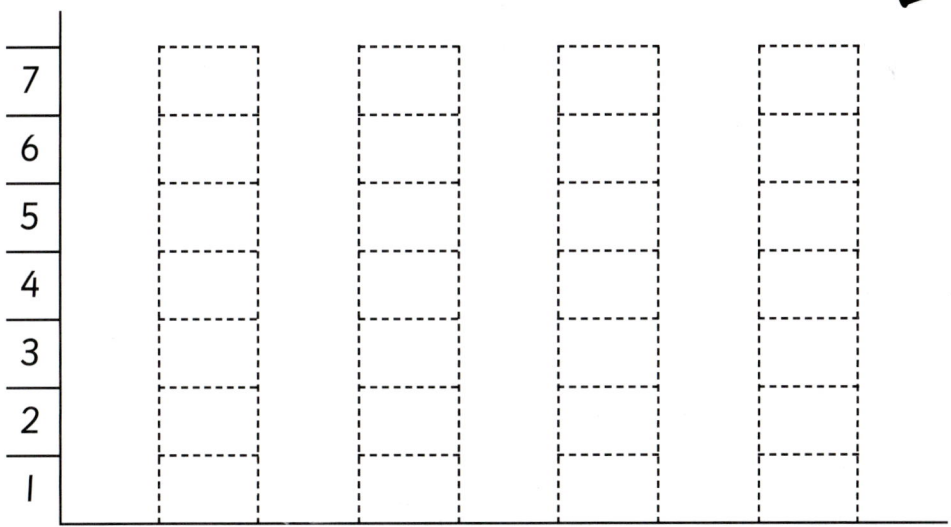

   shape

Time for a sticker, I think.

Tens and units

Write down the number of cubes.

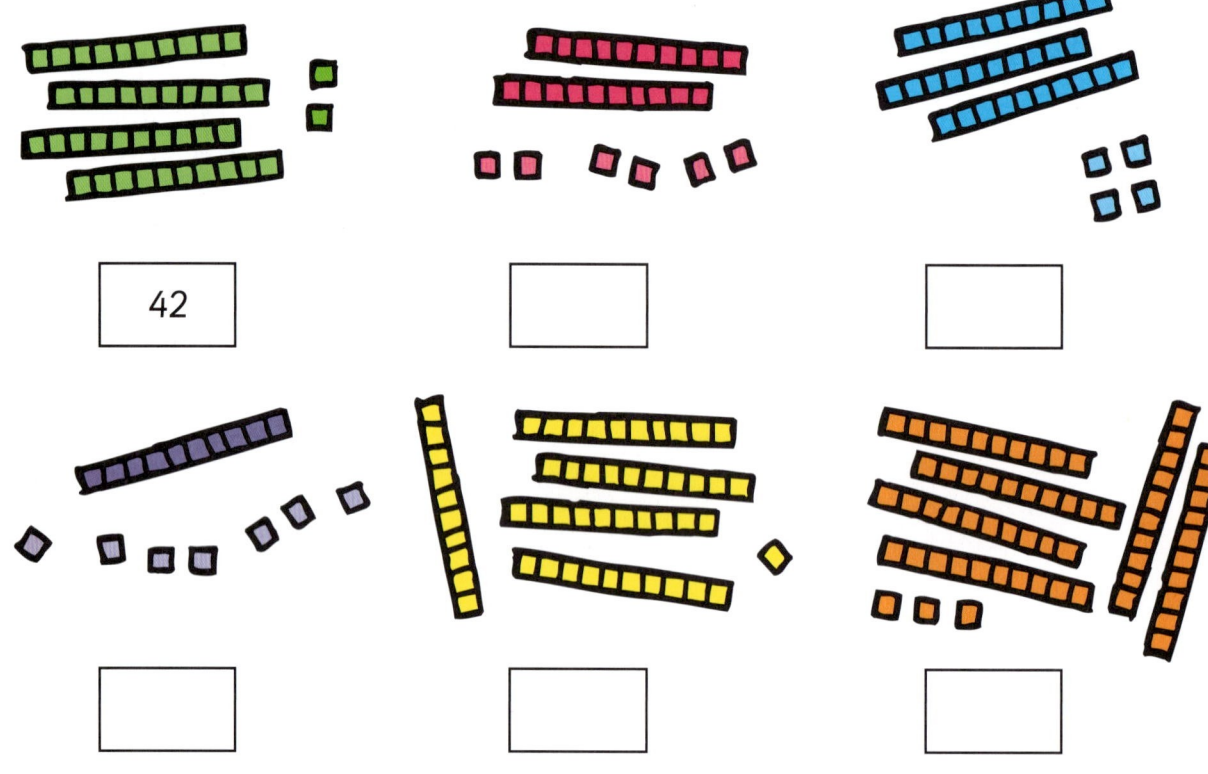

42

Write down how much.

33 p

Great number work!

Tens and units

Write the number shown on each abacus.

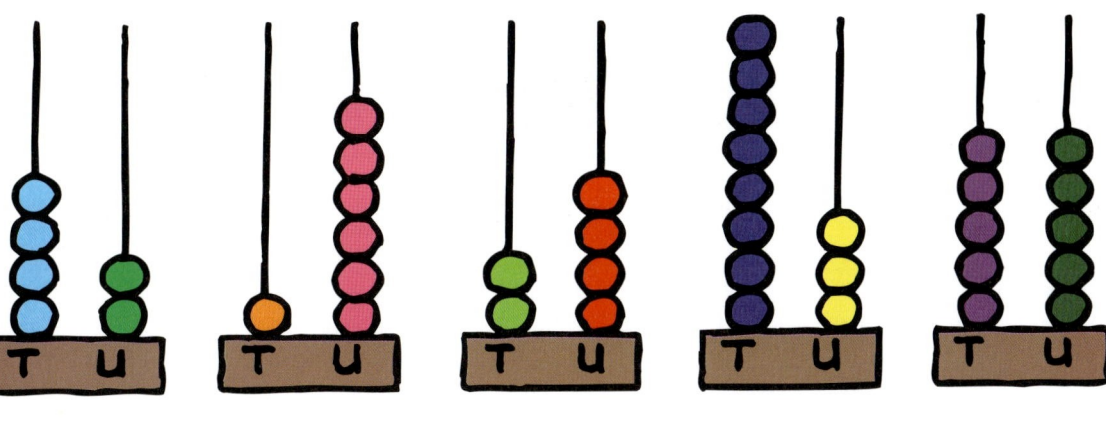

| 42 | | | | |

Draw the beads for each abacus.

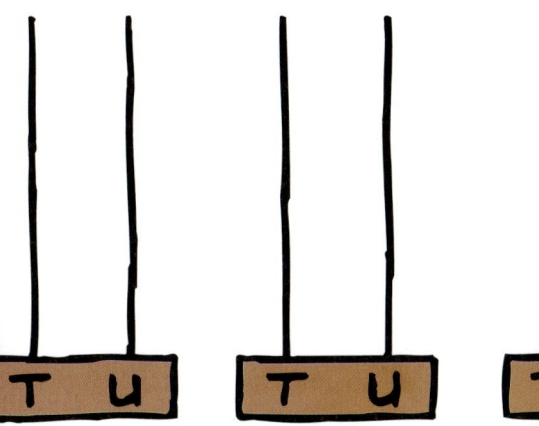
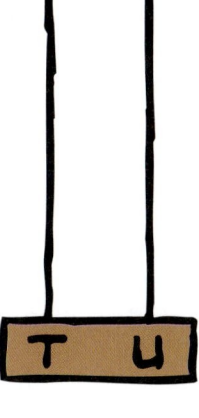
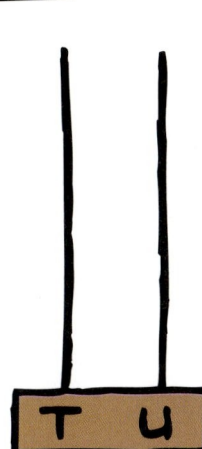

| 23 | 31 | 57 | 60 | 15 |

Note for parents: Remind your child to start with the tens, not the units.

Two-digit numbers

Write these in numerals.

twenty-seven ☐   fifty-six ☐

forty-three ☐   sixty ☐

nineteen ☐   seventy-two ☐

thirty-nine ☐   sixty-eight ☐

fifty-one ☐   eighty-five ☐

Write these in words.

31 ☐   93 ☐

54 ☐   75 ☐

28 ☐   89 ☐

70 ☐   40 ☐

44 ☐   11 ☐

Note for parents: Your child could make a list of parents', grandparents' and siblings' ages.

Shapes

Write the name of each shape. Choose from square, rectangle, circle, triangle.

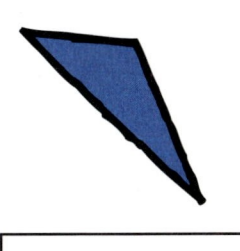 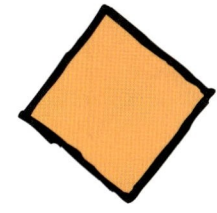 

Colour the rectangles green, the squares red and the triangles blue. Count how many of each.

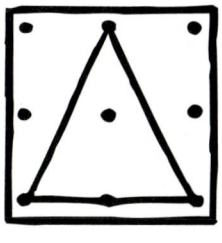 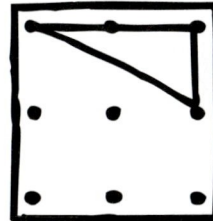  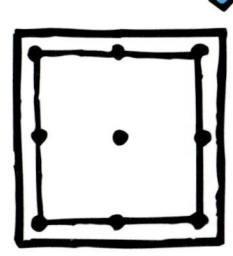

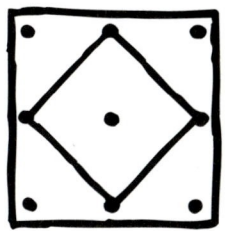 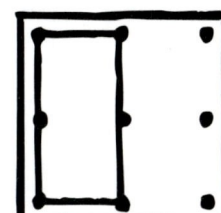 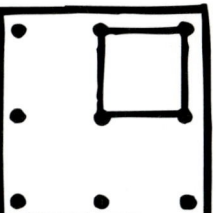 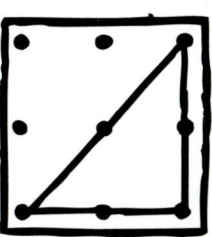

What is your favourite shape?

Shapes

Write the name of each shape. Choose from pentagon, hexagon, rectangle, triangle.

Colour the pentagons yellow and the hexagons red. Pentagons have 5 sides and hexagons 6 sides.

You've really brightened up the page!

Halves and quarters

Colour one half of each shape.

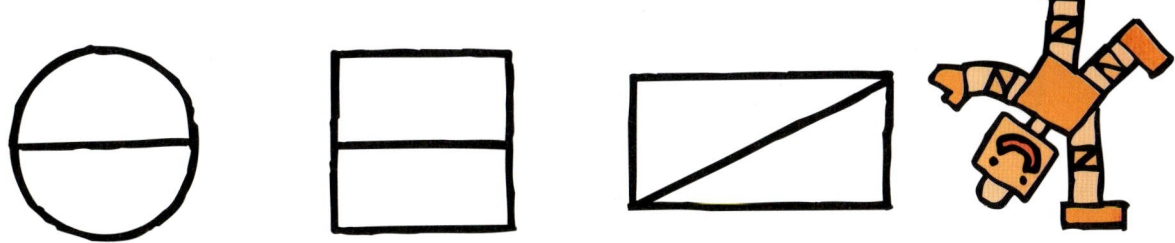

Draw a line to cut each shape in half. Colour the halves.

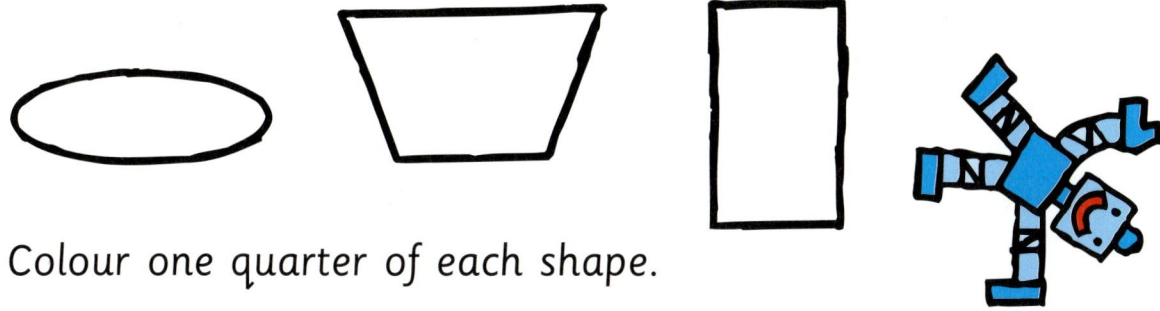

Colour one quarter of each shape.

Draw two lines to cut each shape into quarters.

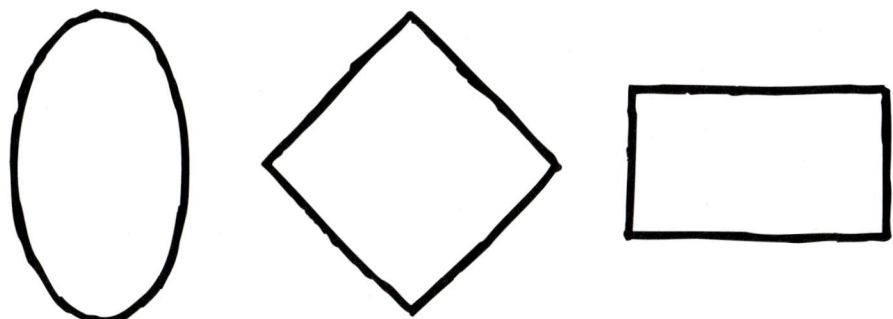

How many quarters are there in a half?

Odds and evens

Write **odd** or **even** for the number of cherries in each bunch.

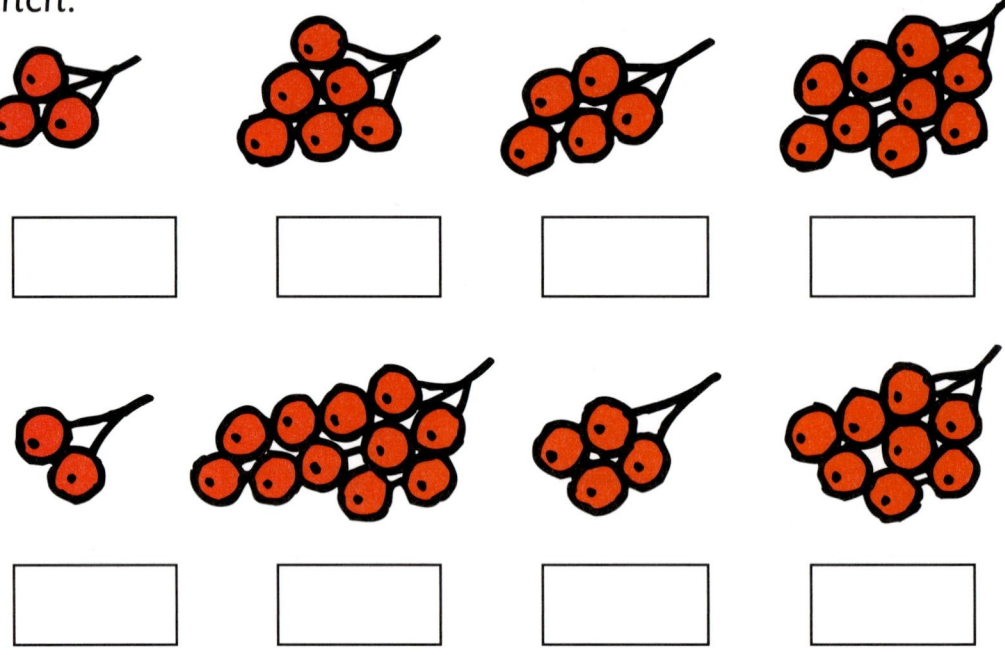

Colour the dominoes:
red if both sides of spots are even
blue if both sides of spots are odd
green if one side is odd and the other side even.

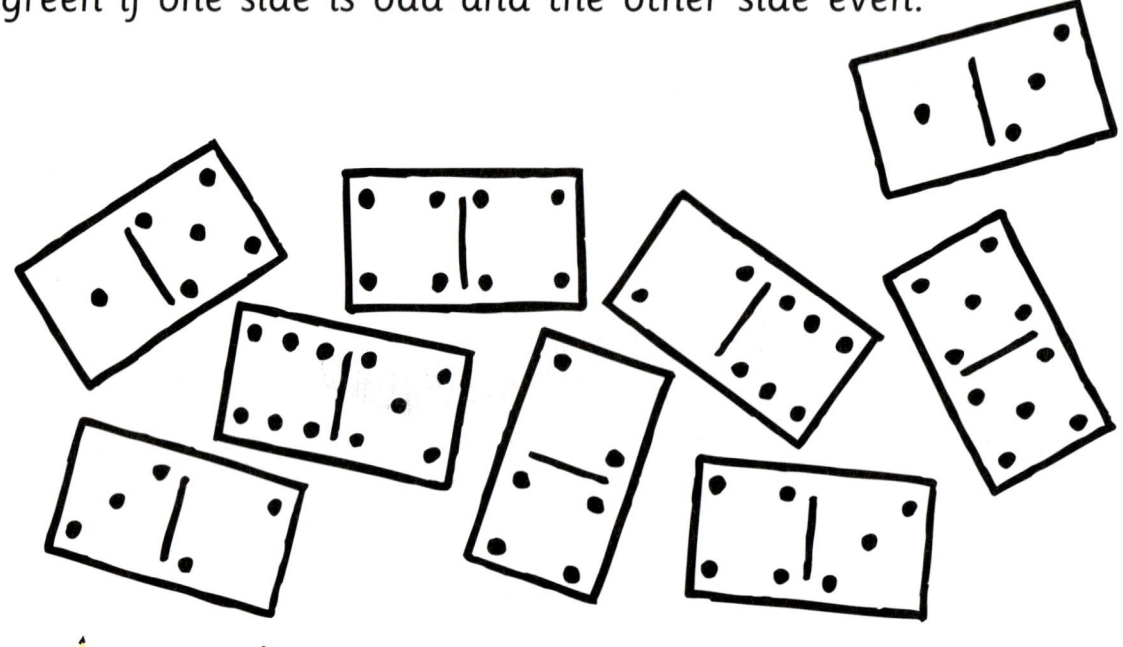

Note for parents: Count odd and even numbers of objects around the home, toys or books, for example.

Hundreds, tens and units

19

Write the number shown.

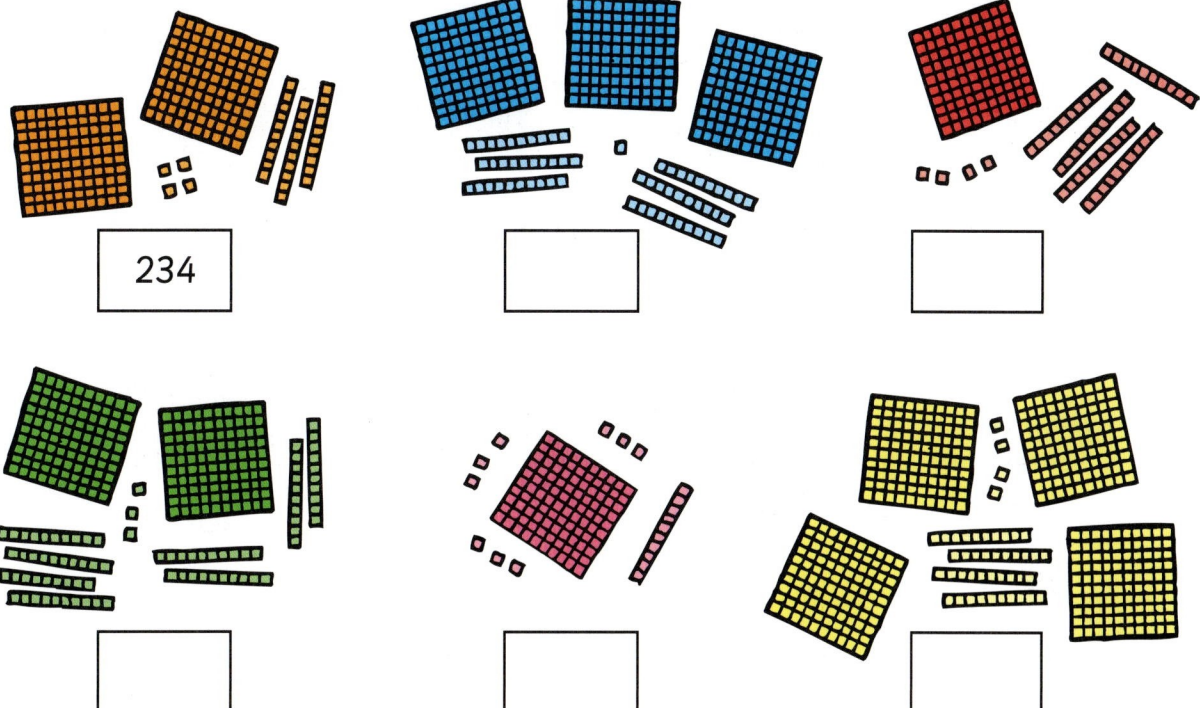

234

Write down how many pence.

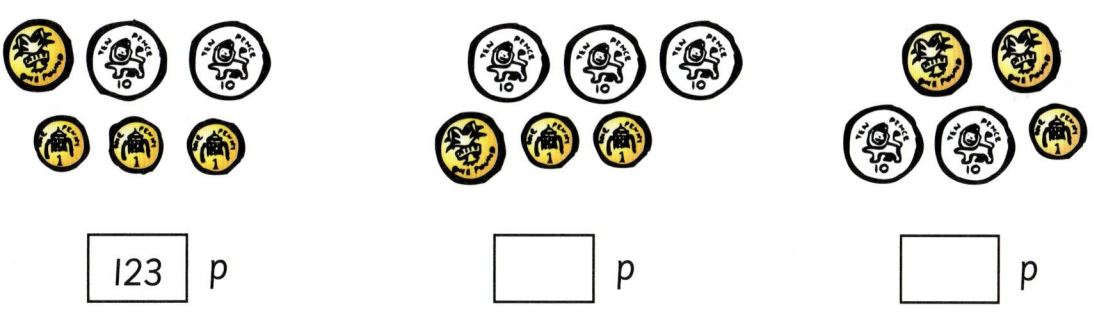

123 p

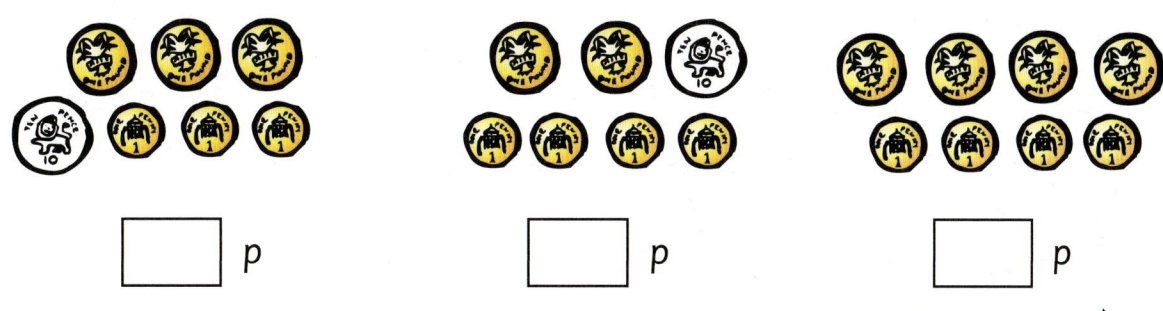

Clever counting, choose a star.

Hundreds, tens and units

Write the number shown on each abacus.

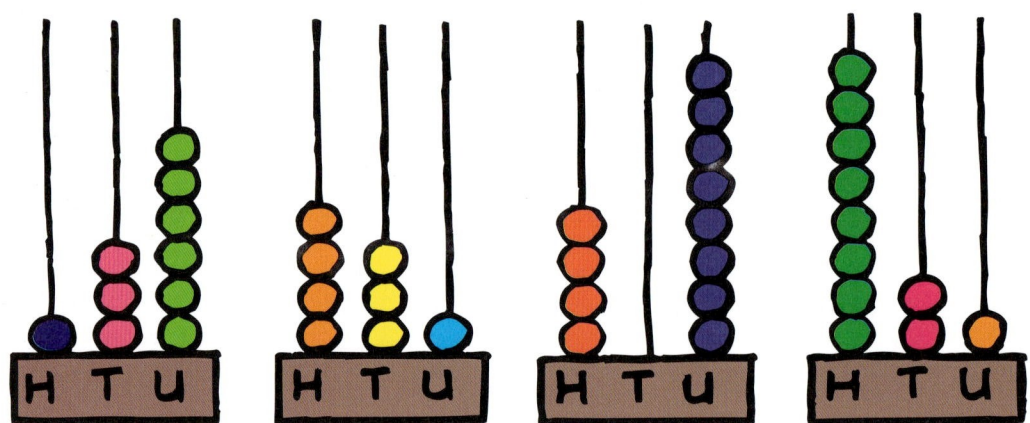

| 136 | | | |

Draw the beads on each abacus.

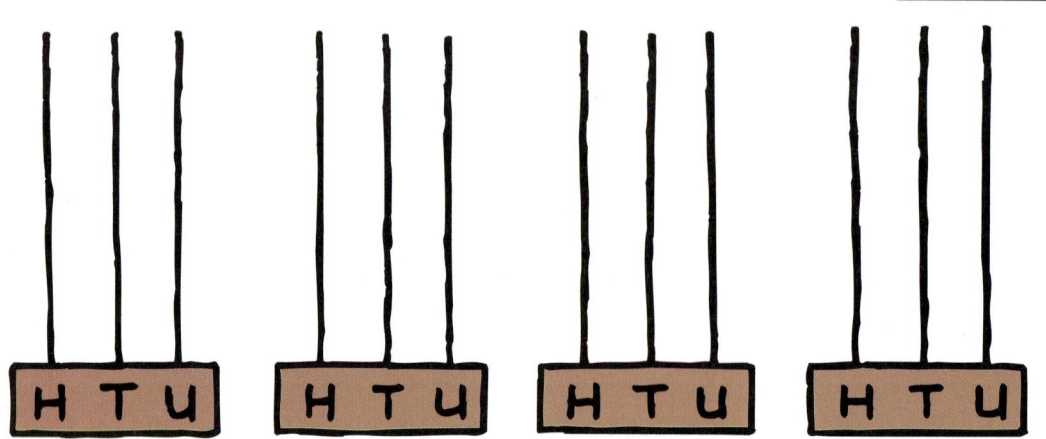

| 551 | 806 | 472 | 163 |

Note for parents: This exercise teaches the relationship between hundreds, tens and units. Start with the hundreds.

Three-digit numbers

Write these in numerals.

two hundred and fifty-one

four hundred and ninety-two

six hundred and seventeen

eight hundred and thirty

five hundred and seventy-four

three hundred and fifty-six

Write these in words.

374

625

942

507

460

224

I can't count all those bugs, can you?

22 Tallies

Write the total of the tally marks for each flavour.

Our favourite ice-cream flavour

	tallies	totals
mint	||||| ||||| ||	
vanilla			
strawberry	||||| ||||| ||||| ||	
chocolate	||||| ||||| |||	

most votes [ ]　　fewest votes [ ]

You will need a die. Throw the die and draw a tally mark for each throw. Stop when one number has been thrown fifteen times. Write the totals.

Die throws

die	tallies	totals
⚀		
⚁		
⚂		
⚃		
⚄		
⚅		

Which flavour would you vote for?

Bar graph

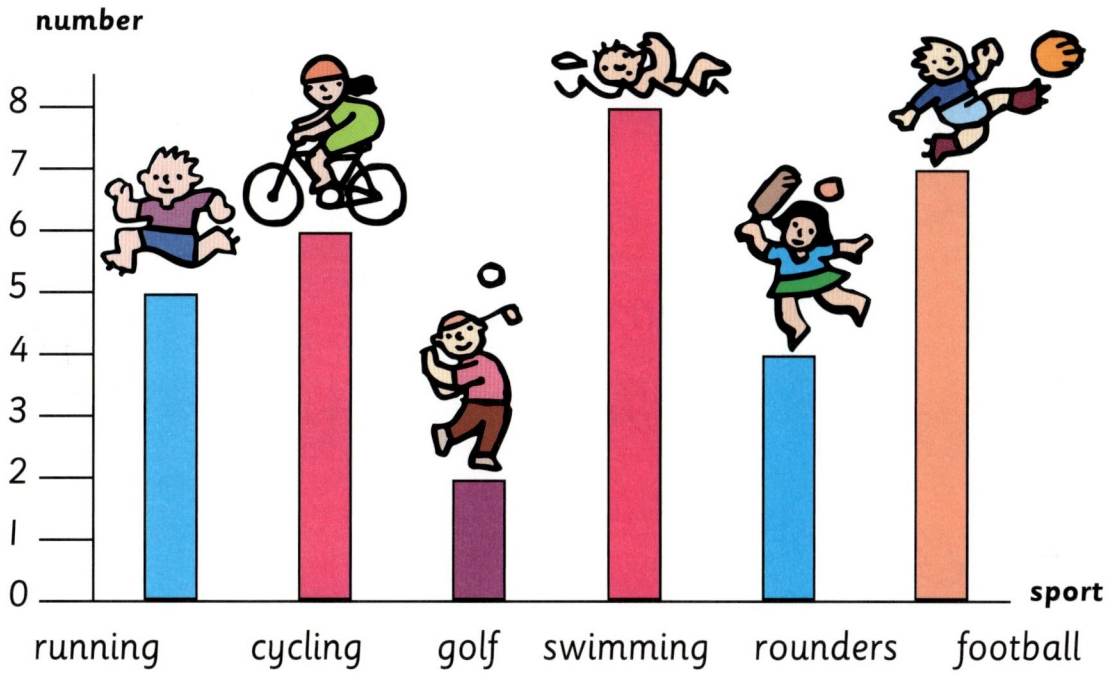

How many voted for: cycling? ☐

rounders? ☐

football? ☐

How many more voted for: swimming than golf? ☐

running than rounders? ☐

football than rounders? ☐

How many people voted altogether? ☐

What is your favourite sport?

24 Halves

Colour one half of each set.

 one half of 8 is 4

 one half of ☐ is ☐

 one half of ☐ is ☐

one half of ☐ is ☐

Write one half of each of these numbers.

4	10	16	2	14	18	6	20
↓	↓	↓	↓	↓	↓	↓	↓
2							

Excellent work, choose a sticker.

Quarters 25

Colour one quarter of each set.

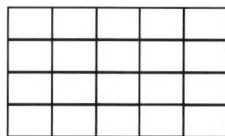 one quarter of  is

one quarter of ▢ is ▢

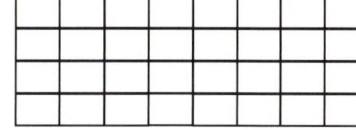 one quarter of ▢ is ▢

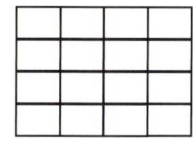 one quarter of ▢ is ▢

Write one quarter of each of these numbers.

12	28	8	24	4	20	16	32
3							

How many quarters make a whole?

26 Time: quarter past, quarter to

Write the time under each clock.

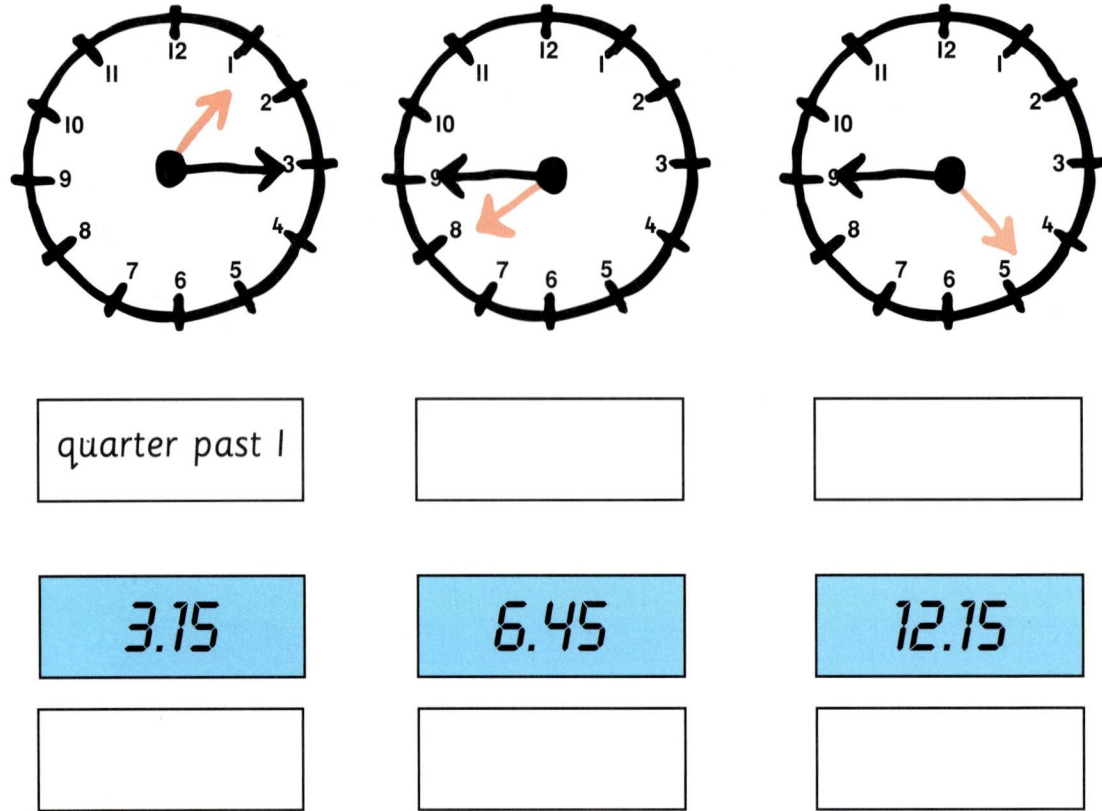

| quarter past 1 | | |

| 3.15 | 6.45 | 12.15 |

| | | |

Draw the hands on the clocks.

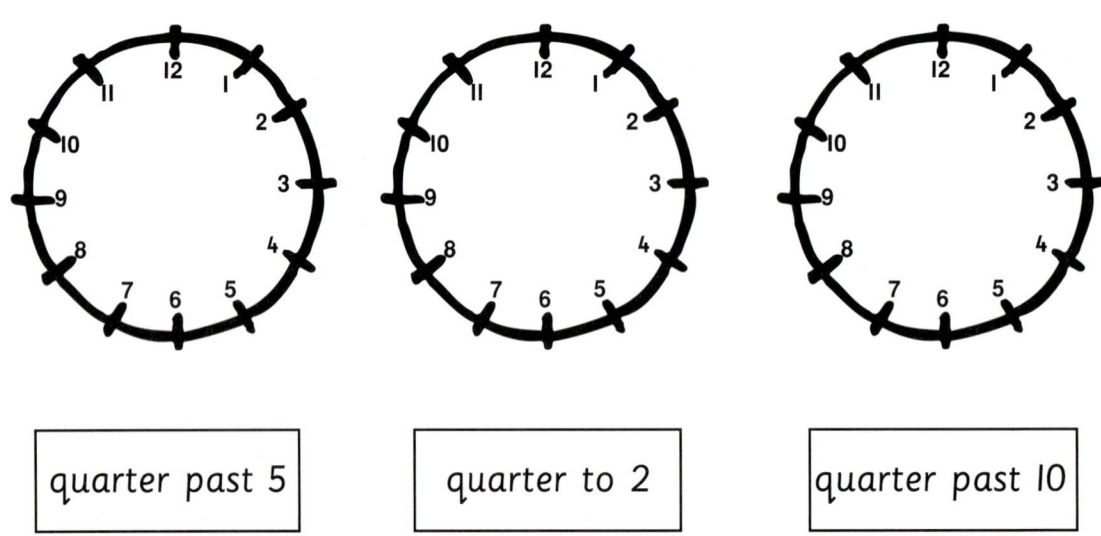

| quarter past 5 | quarter to 2 | quarter past 10 |

Time: five minutes

27

Write the time under each clock.

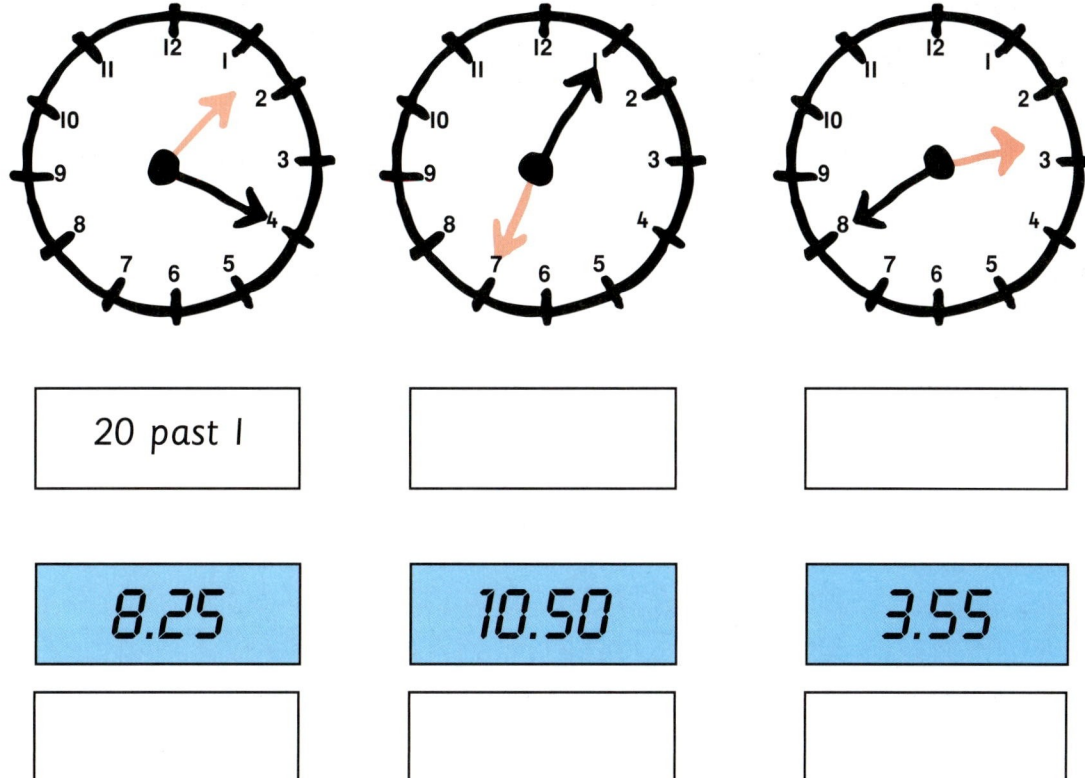

20 past 1

8.25   10.50   3.55

Draw the hands on the clocks.

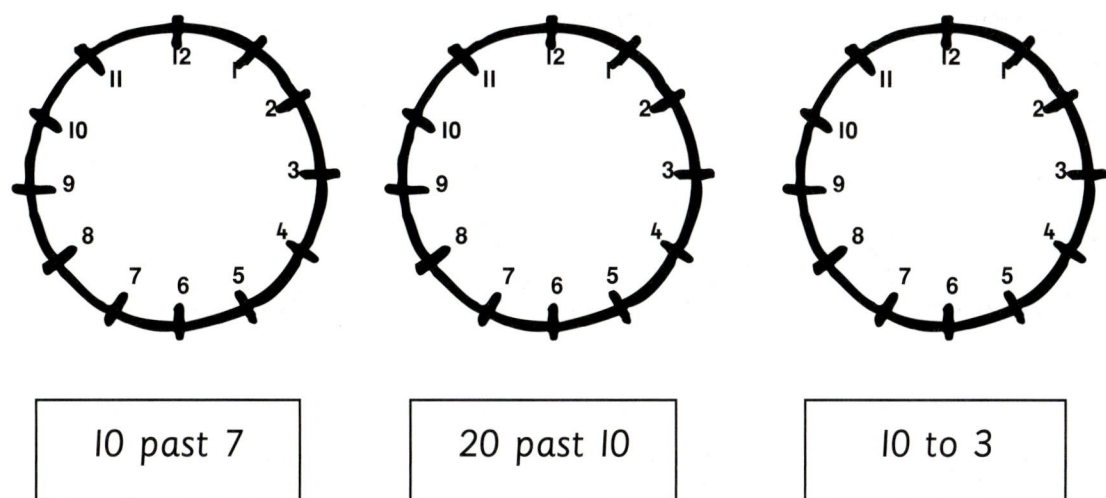

10 past 7   20 past 10   10 to 3

Note for parents: Quarter past, quarter to, and five-minute intervals are tricky to learn. Practise them lots with your child.

Money

Colour **two** coins which make each amount.

Write **three** coins which make these amounts:

 | 20p | 20p | 20p |   | | | |

 | | | |  | | | |

 | | | |  | | | |

Symmetry

Are these shapes symmetrical, yes or no?

Draw the fold lines of symmetry on these shapes.

Which has the most lines of symmetry?

30 Number lines

Write the position of each letter on the line.

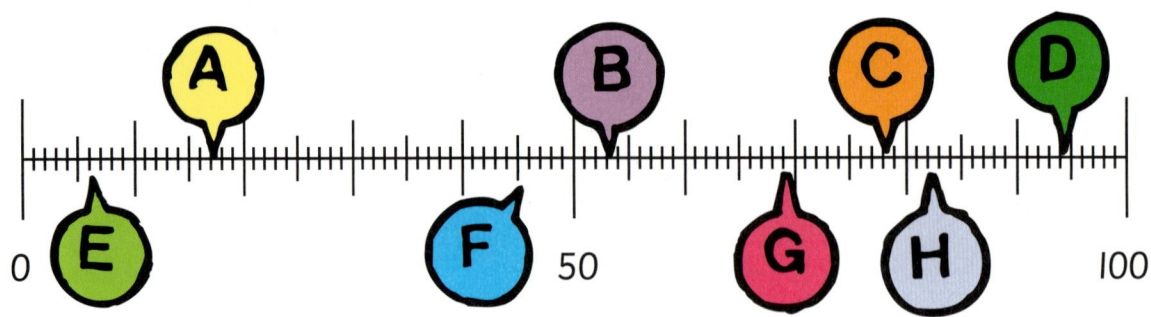

A = | 17 | B = | | C = | | D = | |

E = | | F = | | G = | | H = | |

Mark the position of each letter on the line.

A = 117   B = 145   C = 171   D = 193
E = 108   F = 129   G = 154   H = 180

Mark your age on the first number line.

Shapes

Write the name of each shape.
Choose from cube, cuboid, sphere.

Write down the number of cubes needed to build each of these cuboids.

Did you answer all the questions?

Shapes

Write the name of each shape.
Choose from cone, cylinder, pyramid.

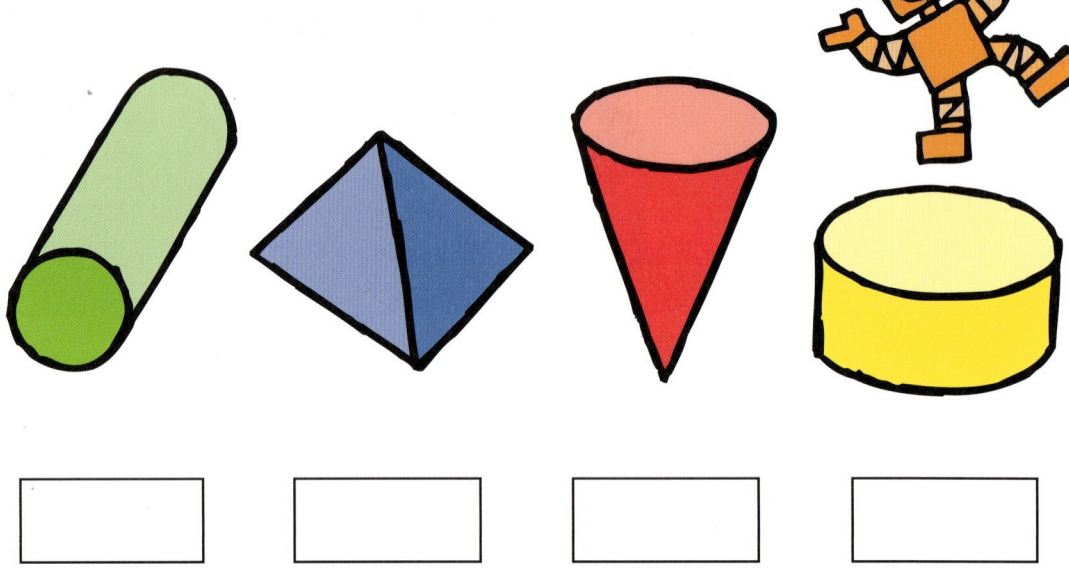

Colour these shapes yellow. Draw a copy of each shape beside it, then colour in your drawings.

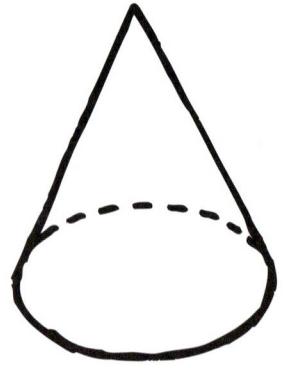   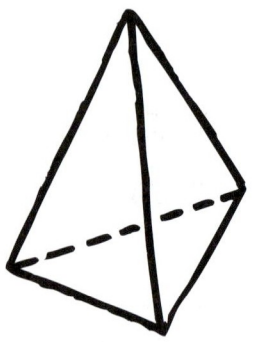

Can you make a cone and a cylinder from a sheet

Note for parents: Can your child recognise and name cones, cylinders and pyramids?